COFFEE

1011
0110
1110

CODE

~~SLEEP~~

REPEAT

Name :

Phone :

Address :